AF317027

THE MEDITATOR

By

Apostle Marvin Thompkins

Dedication:

A tribute to my mom

Table of Contents

I am sharing this writing to inspire someone to understand the power of meditation and how it can change your life. Most of us live in a chaotic, rushed world, where we are either rushing in or out. Deadlines from work, children, school, not to mention all the bad stuff we see daily and hear on social media, in the newspaper, and on television and radio. The world seems so noisy, so loud. Maybe you are seeking a solitary place where you have not been able to find the peace you need to live a happy and productive life, for you, your family, and the world around you. That place that you long for is the presence that is not known to many people.

I first discovered the power that comes from meditating some years ago, maybe 2009-2010. I was very involved in a job that caused me to travel a lot, and my wife and family were not always able to attend. So, after teaching classes at conventions all day and attending meetings and conferences, exhausted, I go back to my room, watch television, but I can't fall asleep.

I am going to be open and honest: sometimes, even when I attempt to read God's word and study, distractions seem to come left and right. I would have a hard time reading the Bible, trying to stay awake and focused. So, as I lie, I flip through the TV channels and find one playing meditation music. I lay there and listen; I allow the music and the sound to enter my mind and body. The next thing I know, it's morning. I feel well rested, and there is a peace and calm in the room.

Since that day in the Hotel Suite in downtown Detroit, I have been practicing meditation ever since. I often sleep listening to scriptures/ prayers or just meditation music. Or just the sounds of nature, or sometimes frequency-meditation music.

I used to have bad dreams and sometimes nightmares, but meditating has given me a strength and a power I never knew existed. It took me to a place people often seek after: a separation from all the noise and chaos of the world. And shows me a place right within me, a place called peace. A place where I can feel safe and at peace, a place where negative powers have no power, and a place where negativity and evil are not invited.

Meditation has become so much a part of my life, almost more than prayer; I am not discouraging anyone from praying, for indeed, there are benefits from doing so. I have been taught that there is power in prayer, but no one taught me the power of meditation. I believe that prayer is when the individual is doing something. Still, meditating is something different, like a "sacred place of separation" where the natural and the supernatural meet, and converse with one another.

Before I get into the actual writing of this, I must say that it was because of an invitation, through meditation, from GOD to enter HIS presence, to be near HIS SPIRIT. I accepted the invitation; I sat and waited to hear HIS voice. I wait for instructions. I have been here in meditation with him before, where I have received peace, divine messages, warnings, and even instructions, so I sit and wait. And yet I know that I am not alone. HIS presence, HIS being, HIS spirit is here, afraid out of a reverence and respect, but also a joy of HIS presence.

And finally, I hear a voice, and it says, "Marvin, write the book! I want you to write and reveal parts of me to the readers that I have selected to know and to understand things pertaining to me."

I say, "YES, LORD, but what do you want me to say? Where do I start?"

"At the beginning," is what I heard.

The word of God says many things about meditation and the rewards it can bring. It is an invitation to be his guest in his quiet spiritual pavilion. I will take you on my journey with the person who wants to reveal somethings clearly seen but often ignored. HE is everywhere, and he is in all places, and all things created are connected to him. Now let us meditate, clear our minds, and open our ideas to those different from our own.

But why is meditation so important? Because spirits are always at war for our minds.

Take a closer look and see what the bible says about the mind:

Romans 12:2 – *"And be not conformed to this world: but be ye transformed by the renewing of your mind, that ye may prove what is that good, and acceptable, and perfect, will of God."*

The mind must be renewed from a system designed to control what and how we think.

2 Corinthians 10:5 – *"Casting down imaginations, and every high thing that exalteth itself against the knowledge of God, and bringing into captivity every thought to the obedience of Christ;"*

The mind must have the correct information to dispel the lies of evil spirits and even Satan, who lies and distorts man's knowledge and truth concerning God.

Isaiah 26:3 – *"Thou wilt keep him in perfect peace, whose mind is stayed on thee: because he trusteth in thee."*

The mind that is constantly thinking about God will find perfect peace.

Philippians 4:8 ESV – *"Finally, brothers, whatever is true, whatever is honorable, whatever is just, whatever is pure, whatever is lovely, whatever is commendable, if there is any excellence, if there is anything worthy of praise, think about these things."*

You must feed your mind, the word of God, honest, right thinking, pure, and positive things. You must protect your eye gates and ear gates from what you see and hear. Music and even visual things that promote sex, violence, murder, hatred, and propaganda should be avoided.

<u>**Romans 8:7 ESV**</u> – *"For the mind that is set on the flesh is hostile to God, for it does not submit to God's law; indeed, it cannot."*

If you do not control your mind, it will control you. And it hates to submit to any power other than its own. You must master it, or it will master you.

It means not letting your own mind and thoughts become your own worst enemy, where it controls emotions that you are expected to master, such as power, greed, anger, murder, temptations, jealousy, wrath, strife, evil communication, murder, suicide, revenge, etc.

The greatest weapon that anyone can use against another human being is to control the mind. Where the mind goes, the body is almost certain to follow. The enemy knows that we all have free will and a conscience to make our own choices. But the world society and evil forces try to control the narratives we are told, that God hates, kills, and murders innocent people, allows babies to be harmed, and loves punishing us. Not True.

Meditation

The mind is an area that Satan constantly tries to control, so Ephesians 6:17 tells us to take the helmet of salvation and the sword of the Spirit, which is the word of God. The helmet protects the Head (Mind thoughts).

Psalms 1:2 – *"But his delight is in the law of the LORD; and in his law doth he meditates day and night."*

You must read the word of God every day, and if you cannot read it, use meditation music with scripture to feed your inner man.

Psalms 49:3 – *"My mouth shall speak of wisdom; and the meditation of my heart shall be of understanding."*

Meditation brings wisdom!

Matthew 6:6 – *"But thou, when thou prayest, enter into thy closet, and when thou hast shut thy door, pray to thy Father which is in secret; and thy Father which seeth in secret shall reward thee openly."*

Meditation is your personal emails to God; blessings are the answers to those emails and prayers.

Psalms 119:11 – *"Thy word have I hid in mine heart, that I might not sin against thee."*

Meditating on God's word will keep you from sinning! And convicts you when you do, and will GPS your way back to repentance when you're lost and have gotten off track.

Psalms 119:99 – *"Oh how love I thy law! it is my meditation all the day."*

Meditation helps keep one focused!

Psalms 63:6 – *"When I remember thee upon my bed, and meditate on thee in the night watches."*

Meditation helps calm the spirit and bring peace and rest to your sleep! As it was in my case.

<u>JOB 15:4</u> – *"Indeed, you do away with reverence, and hinder meditation before God."*

Meditation is an invitation to worship! And keeps you connected to God.

Meditation is an Instruction

Joshua 1:1-9 Context NKJV

God instructs Joshua, the servant of Moses and the new Leader of his people!

This book of the law shall not depart out of thy mouth; but thou shalt meditate therein day and night, that thou mayest observe to do according to all that is written therein: for then thou shalt make thy way prosperous, and then thou shalt have good success. 9, Have I not commanded you? Be strong and of good courage; do not be afraid, nor be dismayed, for the LORD your GOD is with you wherever you go,"

God said to Joshua, "If you want to prosper and have good success and know my thoughts and my ways, then you must meditate on my laws and my commandments. He also commits to being with him to protect him and to be his traveling companion. Imagine GOD stating that he will walk with you? Imagine knowing that you have the biggest and toughest father always with you to keep an eye on you and protect you from everything that comes to try and harm you.

How about you, reader? Is God the Father inviting you to a deeper, more personal place with him so he can reveal himself to you? Maybe he has been just waiting for you to seek him out and find him. I believe I was invited to this place on March 1, 2023. It was 4 am in the morning. I woke up, just about to shower and get ready for the day, but I almost couldn't move. I awakened in meditation. The Creator has something to say!

I sit here still and try to humble myself as best I can, mentally, emotionally, and spiritually. I had just been meditating on the thought that sometimes we must come into God's presence, not do all the talking and all the requesting, but just be in the moment with him and seek what is on HIS mind and HIS heart. I sit in total silence, meditating, blocking everything out. I dare not speak; I sense he does not want me to talk, but to listen. He wants to take me on a journey of meditation. Prayer, I think, is speaking to God, but meditation, I believe, is when God speaks back to us if we can just be still, silent, and attentive.

I sit, I listen, I hear Marvin write the book! I want my people to understand things about me that have been confusing, and I will tell you what to write. I have put my thoughts in your mind for what I want you to write.

I HEAR!

God of the Material Universe

I AM the God of the MATERIAL UNIVERSE: God's kingdom ruleth overall.

By the creation of the material Universe, I mean the creation of the heavens and the earth, and all things originally created therein. Moses said his work is perfect (Deut 32:4); David said His work is perfect (1 Sam 22:31); Solomon said that God made everything beautiful in his time (Eccl 3:1).

The word "Heaven" in Hebrew means Shamayim, meaning lofty, sky, or the higher ether where the celestial bodies revolve. In the book of Job 38: verses 4-7, that the spirit world of angels, Seraphim, Cherubim, and other created beings were created before the earth, for the sons of God were present and shouting together when God laid the foundation of the earth.

Genesis tells us that, in the work of the six days, God with his hands formed each of the living creatures and man out of the dust of the ground (Gen 1:20-27; 2:7-25; Job 26:13; Rom. 9:20). It is only not clear who created the heavens and the earth and all things" In the beginning." Or each in its own period, but it is also clear that God formed all things with HIS hands. God formed light and darkness (Isa 45:7). He did not do this on the first day of Gen 1:3-5, for at that time He merely divided them. Therefore, they must have been created and formed on the first day. It is also stated that God with HIS hands formed "the earth" (Ps, 8;3), "the heavens" (Ps. 19:1), "the planets" (Heb.1:10), and all things (Prov. 26:10).

It is clear from the word of God that the materials were brought into existence, and then, by His hands, He formed them into various parts of the universe. That is, as God spoke, the materials came into existence, and as they materialized, He used them to form all things with His hands, as stated in scripture. (Ps.8:3, 2 Pet. 3-9; Prov. 26:10)

Although we read in scripture 2 Peter 3:8 New King James Version[8] ***But, beloved, do not forget this one thing, that with the Lord one day is as a thousand years, and a thousand years as one day***. It is clear when the bible says in the beginning God created the heaven and the earth, it was not "six thousand years ago God created the heavens and earth as many believers generally teach, the bible say he did it in six days no other than God knew time before it existed. But we do know that God took one day to divide the light from the darkness, but we do not know how long he took to create light.

We do know that He took one day to divide the waters, which covered the earth, and restore the firmaments, and one day to restore the world and set bounds to the seas. Therefore, He naturally took a much longer period to originally bring into existence and form the waters, the firmaments, and the earth with its many mountains and valleys.

God took one day to complete the solar system regulations in connection with the earth, but he evidently used more time to originally bring into existence with His hands and form His vast heavens, and all the suns, moons, stars, and planets without number. God took two days to form the bodies of the fish, fowl, beast, man, and woman. He naturally took much longer to originally create and form each inhabitant of the vast heavens and the many animals and inhabitants who originally lived on the Earth during Lucifer's kingdom, long before the chaos of Gen. 1:2 and the six days of Gen. 1:3-2:25, which you will read about later.

In closing on this matter, if God took six days to restore one little planet to a habitable state and form new inhabitants for the earth. He would have naturally taken much longer to create and form the vast universe, with all its innumerable suns, and planets, and their inhabitants.

God created the material universe to be inhabited with intelligence, free moral agents, to whom He could reveal Himself, and who could enjoy all the rich blessings of life and the goodness of the creator forever. God created plant and animal life, as well as all other things necessary for sustaining life in the universe.

The God of the Plant World

<u>**Psalm 104:14:**</u> *"He causes the grass to for the cattle, And the vegetation for the service of man, that he may bring forth food from the earth."*

Matthew 6:28-30

28 "So why do you worry about clothing? Consider the lilies of the field, how they grow; they neither toil nor spin; 29 "and yet I say to you that even Solomon in all his glory was not arrayed like one of these 30" Now if God so clothes the grass of the field, which today is, and tomorrow is thrown into the oven, will He not much more clothe you, O you of little faith?"

<u>**Genesis 1:29:**</u> *"God clothe the earth with its seasons."*

29 "And God said, 'See, I have given you every herb that yields seed which is on the face of all the earth, and every tree whose fruit yields seed; to you it shall be for food."

God provides all that he has created with food that comes from HIS other creations.

Genesis 2:16-17

16 "And the LORD God commanded the man, saying 'Of every tree of the garden you may freely eat; 17 'but of the tree of the knowledge of good and evil you shall not eat, for in the day you eat of you shall surely die."

God is not responsible for the evil and bad things in the world, Man is! Man had free choice.

Psalms 65: 9-13

9 *"You visit the earth and water it, You greatly enrich it; The river of God is full of water; You provide their grain, For so You have prepared it10You water its ridges abundantly, You settle it furrows; You make it soft with showers, You bless its growth11 You crown the year with your goodness, And your paths drips with abundance.12They drop on the pastures of the wilderness, And the little hills rejoice on every side.13 The pastures are clothed with flocks; The valley also are covered with grain; The shout for joy, they also sing."*

God is a Gardener and caretaker of the earth.

Leviticus 26:3-10:

3 *"If you walk in My statutes and keep my commandments, and perform them,4 then I will give you rain in its season, the land shall yields its produce, and the trees of the field shall yield their fruit.5 Your threshing shall last till the time of vintage shall last till the time of sowing;6 I will give peace in the land, and you shall lie down, and none will make you afraid; I will rid the land of evil beasts, and the sword will not go through the land.7You will chase your enemies and they shall fall by the sword before you8Five of you shall chase a hundred, and a hundred of you shall put ten thousand to flight; your enemies shall fall by the sword before you."*

Obedience can control our economy and the stock market it can stop Wars and protect us from enemies foreign and domestic.

Psalm 67-6

6 *"Then the earth shall yield her increase; God, our own God, shall bless us."*

Obedience can address starvation and food shortages everywhere. Obedience can solve all agricultural problems and produce fresh fruits and vegetables.

Psalms 104:14

14 *"He causes the grass to grow for cattle, and vegetation for the service of man, that he may bring forth food from the earth."*

Obedience can bless the farmers and bring employment for men everywhere.

The God of the Animal World

The same God also provides for what He creates, as stated in **Job 38:39-41**:

39 *"Can you hunt for the prey for the lion, or satisfy the appetite of the young lions, 40When they crouch in their dens, or lurk in their lairs to lie in wait? 41Who provides food for the ravens, when its young one's cry to God, and wonders about for lack of food?"*

God even hears the animals and provides food for them.

Psalms 145:10-16

10 *"All your works shall praise You, Oh Lord And your saints shall bless you."*

11 *"They shall speak of the Glory of your kingdom, and talk of Your power."*

12 *"To make known to the sons of men His mighty acts, And the glorious majesty of His kingdom."*

13 *"Your Kingdom is an everlasting kingdom, and your dominion endures throughout all generations."*

14 *"The Lord upholds all who fall and raises up all who are bowed down."*

15 *"The eyes of all looks expectantly to You, and you give them their food in season."*

16 *"You open your hand and satisfy the desire of every living thing."*

Verse 16 says it best God satisfies the desire of every living thing.

The God of the Spirit World

I hope the reader is now beginning to understand the magnitude of God and the responsibility he carries for maintaining balance, law, and order in all things. The governing power of God is so large and goes way beyond our imagination. To think we have the capacity to narrow God in the Human brain and imagination is useless, because he created the brain we have and can allow us to learn as much as he chooses us to know. I imagine God must laugh when humans try to put him in categories that fit our reasoning, not even once thinking that we draw conclusions based on limited information. So far, we see that God is responsible for the providence of the Material Universe, the Vegetative and Animal World.

Now we explore the God of the Spirit world, beginning in the book of **Isaiah 6:1-7**. The first is called the *"Seraphim."*

Isaiah is commissioned

1. In the year that King Uzziah died, I saw the Lord, high and exalted, seated on a throne; and the train of his robe filled the temple.

2. Above him were *seraphim*, each with six wings: With two wings they covered their faces, with two they covered their feet, and with two they were flying.

3. And they were calling to one another: "Holy, holy, holy is the LORD Almighty; the whole earth is full of his glory."

4. At the sound of their voices the doorposts and thresholds shook, and the temple was filled with smoke.

5. "Woe to me!" I cried. "I am ruined! For I am a man of unclean lips, and I live among a people of unclean lips, and my eyes have seen the King, the LORD Almighty."

6. Then one of the *seraphim* flew to me with a live coal in his hand, which he had taken with tongs from the altar.

7. With it he touched my mouth and said, "See, this has touched your lips; your guilt is taken away and your sin atoned for."

They had wings, Hands, feet, voices, and knowledge.

Cherubim

The next witness I will call to testify is Ezekiel, the Prophet. According to the Ezekiel account as written in scripture found in **Ezekiel 1:5-28**

5. and in the fire was what looked like four living creatures. In appearance their form was human,

6. but each of them had four faces and four wings.

7. Their legs were straight; their feet were like those of a calf and gleamed like burnished bronze.

8. Under their wings on their four sides they had human hands. All four of them had faces and wings,

9. and the wings of one touched the wings of another. Each one went straight ahead; they did not turn as they moved.

10. Their faces looked like this: Each of the four had the face of a human being, and on the right side each had the face of a lion, and on the left the face of an ox; each also had the face of an eagle.

11. Such were their faces. They each had two wings spreading out upward, each wing touching that of the creature on either side; and each had two other wings covering its body.

12. Each one went straight ahead. Wherever the spirit would go, they would go, without turning as they went.

13. The appearance of the living creatures was like burning coals of fire or like torches. Fire moved back and forth among the creatures; it was bright, and lightning flashed out of it.

14. The creatures sped back and forth like flashes of lightning.

15. As I looked at the living creatures, I saw a wheel on the ground beside each creature with its four faces.

16. This was the appearance and structure of the wheels: They sparkled like topaz, and all four looked alike. Each appeared to be made like a wheel intersecting a wheel.

17. As they moved, they would go in any one of the four directions the creatures faced; the wheels did not change direction as the creatures went.

18. Their rims were high and awesome, and all four rims were full of eyes all around.

19. When the living creatures moved, the wheels beside them moved; and when the living creatures rose from the ground, the wheels also rose.

20. Wherever the spirit would go, they would go, and the wheels would rise along with them, because the spirit of the living creatures was in the wheels.

21. When the creatures moved, they also moved; when the creatures stood still, they also stood still; and when the creatures rose from the ground, the wheels rose along with them, because the spirit of the living creatures was in the wheels.

22. Spread out above the heads of the living creatures was what looked something like a vault, sparkling like crystal, and awesome.

23. Under the vault their wings were stretched out one toward the other, and each had two wings covering its body.

24. When the creatures moved, I heard their wings, like the roar of rushing waters, like the voice of the Almighty, like the tumult of an army. When they stood still, they lowered their wings.

25. Then there came a voice from above the vault over their heads as they stood with lowered wings.

26. Above the vault over their heads was what looked like a throne of lapis lazuli, and high above on the throne was a figure like that of a man.

27. I saw that from what appeared to be his waist up he looked like glowing metal, as if full of fire, and that from there down he looked like fire; and brilliant light surrounded him.

28. Like the appearance of a rainbow in the clouds on a rainy day, so was the radiance around him. This was the appearance of the likeness of the glory of the LORD. When I saw it, I fell facedown, and I heard the voice of one speaking.

These were the same beings that drove man from the garden of Eden and was assigned to protect the tree of life according to **Genesis 3:24**

24 After he drove the man out, he placed on the east side of the Garden of Eden *cherubim* and a flaming sword flashing back and forth to guard the way to the tree of life.

Pay close attention to verses 27, 28. How can man claim to describe God and give him a race or anything? When the prophet saw what he did, he fell face down in reverence and fear.

Zoa the Living Creatures

The next being are like the Cherubim, but they have only one head, full of eyes before and behind them. They are like the seraphim in that they have six wings, one has the face of a lion, one like a calf, one like a man, and one like a flying eagle, and they cry holy, holy, holy to God all day and night the word translated "Beast" in Revelation when you read the passage means zoa *"living Creatures"* so now here the testimony of John the Revelator in

<u>Revelations 4 versus 6-9</u>

<u>6</u> Also in front of the throne there was what looked like a sea of glass, clear as crystal. In the center, around the throne, were four living creatures, and they were covered with eyes, in front and in back.

<u>7</u> The first *living creature* was like a lion, the second was like an ox, the third had a face like a man, the fourth was like a flying eagle.

<u>8</u> Each of the *four living creatures* had six wings and was covered with eyes all around, even under its wings. Day and night they never stop saying: "'Holy, holy, holy is the Lord God Almighty, 'who was, and is, and is to come."

<u>9</u> Whenever the *living creatures* give glory, honor and thanks to him who sits on the throne and who lives for ever and ever, the 24 Elders bow down and worship HIM.

Are you starting to be convinced that it is impossible to Truly know and understand God, just trying to imagine the Spiritual being is tasking enough.

Please be reminded that these are all the things that HE, GOD has created!

Arch Angel

The word Archangel is found in connection with Christ coming in the air to take out of the world all the living and the dead saints (**1 Thessalonians 4:15-16**). The word *"arch"* means *"Chief."*

15 According to the Lord's word, we tell you that we who are still alive, who are left until the coming of the Lord, will certainly not precede those who have fallen asleep.

16 For the Lord himself will come down from heaven, with a loud command, with the voice of the *archangel* and with the trumpet call of God, and the dead in Christ will rise first.

17 After that, we who are still alive and are left will be caught up together with them in the clouds to meet the Lord in the air. And so, we will be with the Lord forever.

They have peculiar voices, and they set things in motion according to the plan of GOD and when they will return with Christ.

Another one is found in the book of Jude, verse 9.

9 But even the *archangel* Michael, when he was disputing with the devil about the body of Moses, did not himself dare to condemn him for slander but said, "The Lord rebuke you!"

Michael is considered a prince according to the scripture Daniel 12:1

1 "At that time Michael, the great prince who protects your people, will arise. There will be a time of distress such as has not happened from the beginning of nations until then. But at that time your people—everyone whose name is found written in the book—will be delivered.

They have titles and names, and they fight for us according to God's will.

Fight breaks out with The Spirit Beings

7 Then war broke out in heaven. Michael and his angels fought against the dragon, and the dragon and his angels fought back.

8 But he was not strong enough, and they lost their place in heaven.

9 The great dragon was hurled down—that ancient serpent called the devil, or Satan, who leads the whole world astray. He was hurled to the earth, and his angels with him.

Notice, reader, that the message is clear: we are at War with an enemy who likes to conceal himself in the affairs of our world, and he has help! He has an army of spirit beings called angels who fight against us, but remember we have angels also, fighting on our behalf, and something even greater that we will get to later. Remember WE WIN!

It was Michael the Prince who fights for Israel, who came to assist Daniel when the bad angels tried to hinder the answer to his prayer:

20 So he said, "Do you know why I have come to you? Soon I will return to fight against the prince of Persia, and when I go, the prince of Greece will come.

21 but first I will tell you what is written in the Book of Truth. (No one supports me against them except Michael, your prince.

Our relationship with God is important. Few know that fights are being waged in realms we cannot see with the natural eye. Wars over the answers to our prayers and certain requests. Have you ever prayed and thought that God did not hear your prayers? Did you ever imagine that a spiritual being was trying to intercept the answer to your prayers, to cause you to doubt that God is real? And that there is a whole other world beyond what we see with our natural eyes.

For most, this is an unknown, untold spiritual reality that exists!

God sometimes must send Archangels or special messengers to help us understand the things we cannot, as he did with Daniel.

15 While I, Daniel, was watching the vision and trying to understand it, there before me stood one who looked like a man.

16 And I heard a man's voice from the Ulai calling, "Gabriel, tell this man the meaning of the vision."

17 As he came near the place where I was standing, I was terrified and feel prostrate. "Son of man," he said to me, "understand that the vision concerns the time of the end."

As you see, no human can claim to know or understand everything about God and the unseen realm. Satan, the fallen Cherub, aka the Devil, is behind this deception. He is the god of the world, lurking in the spiritual shadows, trying to deceive us and hinder our prayers, and to destroy us.

2 Corinthians 4:3-4

3 And even if our gospel is veiled, it is veiled to those who are perishing. 4 The god of this age has blinded the minds of unbelievers, so that they cannot see the light of the gospel that displays the glory of Christ, who is the image of God.

Who fell from heaven, according to the accounts of another Eyewitness who was there: according to Luke 10:18, The SON saw him fall

18 He replied, "I saw Satan fall like lightning from heaven.

By now you should be starting to understand who is in control as sets things in motion according to HIS own will and pleasure.

HIS Angel

Now accordingly all angel or these created beings cannot be archangels or Chiefs, so who are they and what are their roles? The first one we will deal with is the second person of the Trinity, who appeared to men as a man, or as a messenger of God. He is called *"the angel of the God."*

Let us see what is written and described about him in **Genesis 21:17 NKJV** we read:

17And God heard the voice of the lad. Then the *Angel of the Lord* called to Hagar out of Heaven, and said to her," What ails you, Hagar? Fear not, for God has heard the voice of the lad where he is.

Most churches do not even teach that God has an Angel!

And then there are other scriptures:

Genesis 31:11-13

[11]Then the *Angel of God* spoke to me in a dream, saying, 'Jacob.' And I said, 'Here I am.'[12] And He said, 'Lift your eyes now and see, all the rams which leap on the flocks are streaked, speckled, and gray-spotted; for I have seen all that Laban is doing to you. 13 I am the God of Bethel, where you anointed the pillar and where you made a vow to Me. Now arise, get out of this land, and return to the land of your family."

Genesis 16 9-13

[9]The *Angel of the LORD* said to her, "Return to your mistress, and submit yourself under her hand."[10] Then the *Angel of the LORD* said to her, "I will multiply your descendants exceedingly, so that they shall not be counted for multitude."[11] And the Angel of the LORD said to her:

"Behold, you are with child,

And you shall bear a son.

You shall call his name Ishmael,

Because the LORD has heard your affliction.

12 He shall be a wild man;

His hand shall be against every man,

And every man's hand against him.

And he shall dwell in the presence of all his brethren."

13 Then she called the name of the LORD who spoke to her, You-Are-the-God-Who-Sees; for she said, "Have I also here [f]seen Him who sees me?" 14 Therefore the well was called Beer Lahai Roi; observe, it is between Kadesh and Bered.

Abraham was familiar with the *Angel of the Lord*, for he testifies; In **Genesis 24:40**

40 But he said to me, 'The LORD, before whom I walk, will send His angel with you, and prosper your way; and you shall take a wife for my son from my family and from my father's house.

These men experienced levels of exposure to God, some of us will never experience or understand, but we thank God for their accounted records, let us hear from the Man Moses in Exodus 23 versus 20-24

20 "Behold, I send an Angel before you to keep you in the way and to bring you into the place which I have prepared. 21 Beware of Him and obey His voice; do not provoke Him, for He will not pardon your transgressions; for My name is in Him. 22 But if you indeed obey His voice and do all that I speak, then I will be an enemy to your enemies and an adversary to your adversaries. 23 For My Angel will go before you and bring you in to the Amorites and the Hittites and the Perizzites and the Canaanites and the Hivites and the Jebusites; and I will [e]cut them off. 24 You shall not bow down to their gods, nor serve them, nor do according to their works; but you

shall utterly overthrow them and completely break down their sacred pillars.

And even later in the New Testament, we read the account in Acts 7:30-34.

But Stephens tells of God's Angel in verses 30-34

30 "And when forty years had passed, an *Angel of the Lord* appeared to him in a flame of fire in a bush, in the wilderness of Mount Sinai. 31 When Moses saw it, he marveled at the sight; and as he drew near to observe, the voice of the Lord came to him, 32 saying, 'I am the God of your fathers—the God of Abraham, the God of Isaac, and the God of Jacob.' And Moses trembled and dared not look. 33 'Then the LORD said to him, "Take your sandals off your feet, for the place where you stand is holy ground. 34 I have surely seen the oppression of My people who are in Egypt; I have heard their groaning and have come down to deliver them. And now come, I will send you to Egypt."

Other Angels, just not HIS

So, just to be clear, the term or word "Angel" comes from the Hebrew, and the Greek means "messenger," as described in Matthew 1:20. Notice it reads "an angel" and not "The Angel of the Lord."

20But while he thought about these things, behold an angel of the Lord appeared to him in a dream, saying, Joseph, son of David, do not be afraid to take to you Mary your wife, for that which is conceived in her is of the Holy Spirit.

Notice that the angel came to him in a dream, as we have discussed so far: God rules over the seen and the unseen realms and dimensions. The angel knew that Joseph was afraid and knew exactly what the situation was, and Joseph needed supernatural counsel and guidance, and God gave it to him.

Now, verse 24 is just a s powerful. Let us read.

24Now Joseph, being aroused from sleep, did as the angel of the Lord commanded him and took to him his wife.

Joseph did as the angel commanded him. I think this is a great point to add: men and women sometimes receive instruction from GOD thru HIS messengers, called Angels. It amazes me that they can speak to us in dreams. Who would ever imagine the dream realm is a real reality? God designed us in such a way that HE's able to access our information resource called the brain to communicate His will to us while here on the earth. Sleep can be seen as a meditative state; in that realm, we are able to see and hear what we cannot when we are awake, unless GOD so desires.

"Marvin Write the Book" came to me just as I was waking up, but I was still not totally awake; I awoke in a state of meditation. I have come to experience revelation in dreams and messages from GOD. I sometimes keep having the same dreams until the message is received and understood. I think we all sometimes keep trying until we get it right.

Others had encountered them as well:

1. Two angels came to Sodom in the evening, and in the morning, these angels hastened Lot and his family to escape for their lives and not to look behind.

2 In her first encounter, Hagar was by the fountain of water in the wilderness, and the Angel of the Lord found her and instructed her to, return to her mistress and submit herself to her. He told her she was pregnant, what she should name her son, and the type of man he would be.'

The Angel also met Hagar again in the wilderness when there was no water, and she thought her child would have died. The Angel heard her voice and brought inner strength and hope to her.

3. Angels of God met Jacob on the way after Laban blessed his daughters, departed, and went back to his own place.

4. When the Egyptians, their chariots and horsemen were pursuing the people of Israel after Pharaoh let them go, The Angel of God went before the Israel's camp and went behind them with the pillar of cloud.

5. The Angel of the Lord sat under an oak which was in Ophrah and appeared to Gideon when he was threshing wheat by the winepress. The angel appeared unto him and said, The LORD is with you, you mighty man of valor.

6. An Angel appeared to Manoah's wife, who was barren, and foretold her that she will conceive and bear a son and that she should not drink not wine nor strong drink and eat not any unclean thing. Her son shall be a Nazarite to God from the womb to the day of his death.

7. An angel spoke to Elijah the Tishbite and said, Arise, go up to meet the messengers of the king of Samaria, and say unto them, is it not because there is not a God in Israel, that ye go to enquire of Baalzebub the god of Ekron? (II Kings 1:3) AND angel of the Lord instructed Elijah, 'Go down with him: be not afraid of him. And he arose, and went down with him unto the king.' (II Kings 1:15)

8. Hezekiah the king prayed and cried to heaven and the Lord sent an angel who cut off all the mighty men of valor, and the leaders and captains in the camp of the king of Assyria. So, he returned with shame of face to his own land. (II Chronicles 32:21)

9. Daniel while he was in prayer, the angel Gabriel touched him about the time of the evening offering and talked with him, and said, I am now come forth to give you skill and understanding. He also experienced the angel (one of the chief princes), Michael, helping him when the prince of Persia, Satan, withstood him for 21 days.

BIRTH OF JOHN AND JESUS AND HIS DEATH

10. Angel appeared to Zacharias to deliver a message that he will have a son, what his name will be (John), his calling, and what he shall become.

11. Angel Gabriel sent to the Virgin Mary and exhorted her that she is highly favored of the Lord and that she will bring forth a son and call his name Jesus.

12. Angel also appeared to Joseph in a dream to confirm that Mary will bring forth a son and call his name Jesus.

13. The angel of the Lord came upon country shepherds who watched over their flock by night, to bring them good tidings and announce the birth of a Savior, Christ the Lord.

14. When Mary Magdalene and other Mary went to see the sepulcher, angel of the Lord descended from heaven and rolled back the stone, and told them that, 'He is not here, he is risen from the dead.'

BOOK OF ACTS

15. When the Sadducees and high priest put the Apostles in prison, the angel of the Lord opened the prison doors and brought them out and told them to go, stand, and speak in the temple to the people the words of life.

16. Angel of the Lord spoke to Phillip and told him to go south on the way that goes to Jerusalem to Gaza. When Phillip did go, he met an Ethiopian eunuch who had come to Jerusalem to worship.

17. Cornelius, a centurion, a just man, was instructed by an angel of God in a vision to send men to Joppa and get Simon Peter, who is staying with Simon, the tanner house by the seaside. So, Cornelius did as the angel instructed him. (Acts 10:3-6)

18. When Peter was placed in prison, after James, the brother of John was killed, the angel of the Lord came upon him and a light shined in the prison, smote Peter on the side and raised him up, saying, Arise up quickly. And his chains fell off his hands. (Acts 12:7)

And the angel said to him, to put his garment on and follow him. The angel took him past the first and second wards, then through the iron gate that leads to the city, which opened, and he passed on through one street. Then the angel left.

19. Peter realized that the God sent an angel to deliver him out of the hand of Herod and from all the expectation of the people of the Jews (Acts 12)

20. The ship undergo difficulties during a storm and tempestuous wind, and the crew had no hope, an angel stood by Paul the night, and ministered to him, comforted him, and told him not to fear.

I would be remiss if I said that I have never had angelic encounters, because I've seen them in dreams and have been instructed by them. I have had them deliver me from death several times, so much so that even that could be a book of its own. They have helped keep me from crashing and dying in car crashes, passed out driving moments away from crashing into a light pole. The angel physically touched my shoulder and woke me up in the nick of time. They have been sent to stop my car from crashing while driving on black ice on the expressway, and my car was twirling in circles while oncoming traffic luckily was not close enough to hit my car and kill me, moments away from hitting the wall embankments at a perfect stop.

They have kept me from drowning as a child, they have given me advanced warning not to go certain directions where danger was present, and I believe even on one occasion one was sent to give me a ride in a car on a dangerous, dark road while I was walking one morning.

I have heard them speak to me audibly in dreams and show me signs of GOD in the earth. I am not a special person by no means; there is nothing great or significant about my life. I am a regular person, just like you, reader, just like those in the Bible.

And maybe you, the reader, have had your own experience with them and know them for real.

They are like US.

Now let us get into the character and nature of them:

They are intelligent and wise, according to 2 Samuel 14:20

20 To bring about this change of affairs, your servant Joab has done this thing; but my lord is wise, according to the wisdom of the angel of God, to know everything that is in the earth."

2 Samuel 19: 27

27"And he slandered your servant to my lord the king, but my lord the king is like the angel of God. Therefore, do what is good in your eyes

The King (David) was given wisdom in dealing with God's people and others.

They are patient, according to the story of Balaam in Numbers 22;

22-41 An angel was sent to stand in the way of Balaam and he was riding on his donkey with his two servants accompanying him, the donkey then sees the *Angel of the Lord standing in the way with a sword drawn in his hand*, and the donkey turned aside out of the way and went into the field, so Balaam unaware that an angel has been sent to kill him, hits the donkey to go back the other direction.

So, the angel closed in even more and stood between the narrow path between the vineyard, with a wall on one side and a wall on the other. This time, when the donkey saw the angel of the Lord, she pushed herself up against the wall and crushed Balaam's foot against the wall, so he struck her again. Then the Angel of the Lord went further and stood in a narrow place where there was nowhere to turn either to the right hand or to the left. And when the donkey, who apparently was not taking her eyes off that Angel, saw that the Angel was still there, she lay down under Balaam, so Balaam was even madder and took his staff and struck the donkey.

Now God had seen enough, so he opened the mouth of the donkey to speak, and she said, "What have I done to you, that you have struck me three times? If that was not strange, having the donkey to talk."

Balaam replies, "Because you have abused me. I wish I had a sword in my hand, for now I would kill you!"

The donkey tells him she has been obedient ever since she was his to that day, and had she ever acted that way or hurt you.

Balaam replies," No."

GOD opened his eyes; he saw the angel (armed) and fell on his face.

They Have weapons, and know how to use them!

Notice the scriptures said he had a sword, and it was in his hands to kill him, and the sword was not what most religious people like to make a sword, and that is the word of God, no, this was a real tool used for killing.

Now the Angel of the Lord asked Balaam, "Why have you struck your donkey these three times? Behold, I have come out against you, because your way is perverse before Me. The Donkey saw me and turned aside from Me three times. If she had not turned aside from me surely, I would also have killed you by now, and let her live. What Patience."

The donkey would have lived out of reverence, the human would have died due to ignorance! Perversion brings the wrath of God. Balaam refused to do right; that which was good, he was unreasonable and cranky. He even appears angry and violent; he lashed out at the donkey, his source of transportation.

Most of the emphasis of those scriptures was mine, but I think you get the point. What a story! How many times has God sent something into your life or provided something to help save your life from the pending destruction ahead, and we kick and fight it because we cannot see what is coming? Think of me then as a writing donkey that God is using to warn you to make sure your ways do not cause Him to send His Angel to pay you a little visit; it may be your last if you do not take heed to the pain you have already suffered.

Does your life please God the Creator, or is it filled with only doing the desires of your heart and the satisfying of your flesh, getting high, sexually driven, money, greed, power, for some even murder or worse?

They are Greater in Power

According to 2 Peter 11:

11 *whereas angels, who are greater in power and might,* do not bring a reviling accusation against them before the Lord.

They are joyful according to **Luke 15verse 10:**

10 Likewise, I say to you, *there is joy in the presence of the angels of God over one sinner who repents."*

They are modest, according to **1 Corinthians 11:10.**

10 For this reason the woman ought to have *a symbol of authority on her head, because of the angels.*

They are Holy according to **Mark 8 verse 38.**

38 For whoever is ashamed of Me and My words in this adulterous and sinful generation, of him the Son of Man also will be ashamed when He comes in the glory of His Father with the holy angels."

They are Glorious according to Luke 9:26

26 For whoever is ashamed of Me and My words, of him the Son of Man will be ashamed when He comes in His own glory, and in His Father's, and of the holy angels.

They are Immortal according to Luke 20 verse 36.

36 *nor can they die anymore, for they are equal to the angels and are sons of God, being sons of the resurrection.*

They are heavenly spiritual beings according to **Psalms 104:1-4**

You are clothed with honor and majesty,

2 Who cover Yourself with light as with a garment,

Who stretch out the heavens like a curtain.

3 He lays the beams of His upper chambers in the waters,

Who makes the clouds His chariot,

Who walks on the wings of the wind,

⁴ Who makes His angels spirits,

His ministers a flame of fire.

They traveled with God when he visited Abraham on his way to Sodom and Gomorrah because their perverseness had reached GOD'S attention and he wanted to see for himself, **Genesis 18,** when HE with HIS angels pays a visit to Abraham: **Genesis 18 verses-20-26**

²⁰ And the LORD said, "Because the outcry against Sodom and Gomorrah is great, and because their sin is very grave, ²¹ I will go down now and see whether they have done altogether according to the outcry against it that has come to Me; and if not, I will know."

²² Then the men turned away from there and went toward Sodom, but Abraham still stood before the LORD. ²³ And Abraham came near and said, "Would You also destroy the righteous with the wicked? ²⁴ Suppose there were fifty righteous within the city; would You also destroy the place and not spare it for the fifty righteous that were in it? ²⁵ Far be it from You to do such a thing as this, to slay the righteous with the wicked, so that the righteous should be as the wicked; far be it from You! Shall not the Judge of all the earth do, right?"

²⁶ So the LORD said, "If I find in Sodom fifty righteous within the city, then I will spare all the place for their sake.

How powerful Abraham pleads for the righteous. God spares the wicked sometimes because of the righteous. Being righteous can save the lives of family and friends and even a nation, YOU'RE WELCOME AMERICA!

Reader, maybe you are one of those righteous people that GOD looks to when deciding what to do with things in the world.

Righteousness and holiness pay off. It can determine the outcome of an act of GOD, or prevent one.

Imagine a world without any righteous, no one praying, no one interceding to GOD, praying, seeking forgiveness for the SINS and perversion we have been accused of before GODS throne. And where does the praying for forgiveness of sins for self and other usually happen? The place of the Church. The place where Satan does whatever he can to discourage people from going learning. But I believe GOD visits to see who attends and who does not; who commits themselves to right moral living and standards. They resist perversion and selfish life pleasures.

I pray that an Angel never receives my name; or pays me a visit, because your life is contrary to HIS.

Angels can also:

"Drive spirit horses," according to **Zech. 1:7-11**

"Guard gates," according to **Revelations 21;12**

"Wage war in bodily combat," according to **Revelations 12. 7-9**

"Execute judgements," according to **Genesis 19**

"Minister to saints," according to **Daniel 6:22, Matthew 4:11**

"Help each individual," according to **Matthew 18:10**

"Strengthen in trials, rule nations, sing praise and worship" -**Math 4:11, Dan: 10-11**

"Lead sinners to gospel workers," according to **Acts 10:3**

They "Appear in dreams," "direct preachers **Act 8:26**," "minister before God" ("bind Satan Rev 20"). This one is very important.

"They accompany Christ to the earth."- **Matthew 16:27**

"They witness confessions," **Luke 15, verses 8-9**

"They receive departed spirits," **Luke 16:22**

"They are called watchers," **Daniel 4:13-23**

They are imparting God's will; they are not to be worshipped; they are organized into principalities and powers with thrones of God.

They are innumerable, they are to be judge and ruled by the saints, they are subject to God, they are interested in our affairs as stated earlier, they are being taught wisdom by the church **Ephesians 3:10, 1 Corinthians 4-9**, They look into the things of salvation 1Peter 1-10-12, They observe us **1 Corinthians 4:9**, They can cook **1Kings 19;5-7**, They wear garments **John 20:12**, they appear unaware **Hebrews 13:2**, they have been tested **1Timothy 5:21, Job 4:18**, dwell in heaven **Revelation 12;12** stand before God 2 chronicles 18:18, Christ is better than the Angels **Hebrews 1:5- 2:16**.

You may be sitting there, saying to yourself, "Man, this is a lot to take in and grasp!"

I agree.

Even as I meditate, did you catch that the angels learn from us is worth repeating:

10 to the intent that now the [d]manifold wisdom of God might be made known by the church to the [e]principalities and powers in the heavenly places, 11 according to the eternal purpose which He accomplished in Christ Jesus our Lord, 12 in whom we have boldness and access with confidence through faith in Him. 13 Therefore I ask that you do not lose heart at my tribulations for you, which is your glory.

Now we see why so many attacks are waged against the Church and its Leaders, Teachers, and other offices. It is the place where God reveals the secrets to the hidden things the place where the angels come learn, fellowship, and gather information and reports on our lives and activities for God to assist us against the attacks of our worse enemy, who was once a beautifully created Cherub, who lost his position his power his rule his domain and now seek to take our opportunity away. But be certain he is not alone; he has help. Remember, they are like us, un they have wills. According to Isaiah 14:12-14, it deals with the fall of Lucifer (aka Satan, the Devil). Remember, Jesus said in Luke 10, "He beheld Satan fall as Light to the earth"!

The Fall of Lucifer

Isaiah 14-12-17

O Lucifer, son of the morning!

How you are cut down to the ground,

You who weakened the nations!

[13] For you have said in your heart:

'I will ascend into heaven,

I will exalt my throne above the stars of God;

I will also sit on the mount of the congregation

On the farthest sides of the north;

[14] I will ascend above the heights of the clouds,

I will be like the Most High.'

[15] Yet you shall be brought down to Sheol,

To the lowest depths of the Pit.

[16] "Those who see you will gaze at you,

And consider you, saying:

'Is this the man who made the earth tremble,

Who shook kingdoms,

[17] Who made the world as a wilderness

And destroyed its cities,

Who [f]did not open the house of his prisoners?

Satan does not, nor will he ever Have more Power Than GOD, what he has is very powerful influence, so powerful was his influence he took others angel with him who became rebellious spirits who what are called evil spirits or devils, I think it's safe to allude to the conclusions that if Gods angels can interact and have bearings in this world we live in then it's safe to say that Lucifer, Satan and his demons try to infiltrate the affairs of man as well.

The word "Devil" is used of Satan, the Prince of demons, according to **Matthew 9 32-:34**

32 As they went out, behold, they brought to Him a man, mute and demon possessed. **33** And when the demon was cast out, the mute spoke. And the multitudes marveled, saying, "It was never seen like this in Israel!"

The Demon took the man's voice! But he spoke once it was cast out of the man!

34 But the Pharisees said, "He casts out demons by the ruler of the demons.

Notice again it was the religious people making the wrong interpretation.

Again, we see in **Matthew 12 verse 24**

24 Now when the Pharisees heard it, they said, "This fellow does not cast out demons except by Beelzebub, the ruler of the demons.

The Greek word for devil used in connection with Satan is diabolos, which means adversary, false accuser, slanderer.

There is only one devil, but there are many demons. Satan has Angels, and they are a well-organized, very calculated group that seeks opportunities given to them by Man.

We talked about GODS Kingdom and his angels and created spirits, now we must examine Lucifer's, the devil, and his angels and those who work with him against us.

The Doctrine of Satan

First, we will discuss what he is not. He is not an evil principle, in a red suit with horns and a large pitchfork; he is not an error of the mortal mind, a disease germ, or an abstract power.

The bible tells us he is:

He is a real person. "Satan stood up against Israel, and provoked[enticed] David to number Israel" **1 Chronicles 21:1**

He has access to Heaven and the earth, according to Job 1:6[6] . One day, the angels came to present themselves before the LORD, and Satan also came with them. [7] The LORD said to Satan, "Where have you come from?" Satan answered the LORD, "From roaming throughout the earth, going back and forth on it."

Jesus dealt with him as with a person. Jesus dealt with his temptation for 40 days before Jesus dismissed him, not destroyed him as some teach and believe. Satan has not been destroyed yet! According to **Matthew 4: 1-11**.

Jesus waged war on him as a person and went about destroying the works of the devil and delivering men from his power, **Acts 10:38**

[38] how God anointed Jesus of Nazareth with the Holy Spirit and power, and how he went around doing good and healing all who were under the power of the devil, because God was with him.

Christ taught that Satan was a real person according to **Luke 10:18** *When he said I saw him (Satan) fall from Heaven; and that he was the deceiver of the whole world and the personal leader of the whole world and the personal leader of many angels* **(Rev 12:7-12)**, *one day he (Satan) will give power to Antichrist and receive personal worship* **(Rev 13:1-4)**. *And that he will at fight at Armageddon and will be taken and bound by a chain and cast into a literal prison for 1,000 years* **(Rev 20;1-3)**; *and that he will lead one more rebellion* *against God and then he will be placed in the lake of Fire forever to be tormented* **(Rev.20:7-10)**

The Apostles fought with him as a real person **(Eph 6: 10-18)**.

He opposed Paul as a person **(1 Thes 2:18)** [18] For we wanted to come to you—certainly I, Paul, did, again and again—but Satan blocked our way.

Peter referred to him as a roaring lion, walking about, seeking whom he may devour **(1 Peter 5: 8-9)** [8] Be alert and of sober mind. Your enemy, the devil, prowls around like a roaring lion looking for someone to devour. [9] Resist him, standing firm in the faith, because you know that the family of believers throughout the world is undergoing the same kind of sufferings.

Paul and Peter, and even Christ for that matter, say that they were able to recognize him in Spiritual tactics but in human form!

Paul warns men against a personal devil and tells Saints not to give place to the devil, according to **Ephesians 4:27**: "Do not give the devil a foothold." [28] Anyone who has been stealing must steal no longer, but must work, doing something useful with their own hands, that they may have something to share with those in need.

Believers are admonished to work with their own hands and share with others from the earnings gained from employment, and that is not begging or raising money; it is obedience to the word of God.

Paul goes further in **(Eph: 6:11)** [11] Put on the full armor of God, so that you can take your stand against the devil's schemes.

James says in Chapter 4, verse 7, in his own writings [7] Submit yourselves, then, to God. Resist the devil, and he will flee from you.

Personal conversation was had with him as you see above. God spoke to him in the book of Job 1-6-7 6 One day the angels[a] came to present themselves before the LORD, and Satan[b] also came with them. [7] The LORD said to Satan, "Where have you come from?"

Satan answered the LORD, "From roaming throughout the earth, going back and forth on it."

Remember Peter's warning, "roaring Lion" looking to devour!

He is an angel with a body, soul, spirit like all other angels, he was beautiful, he was seen with a body **(1 Chr 21:1)**, he has a heart **(Isaiah 14:12-14)** he is capable of pride and speech **(Eze 28:17)**, he has a kingdom **(Mrk 3:23-26)** ²² And the teachers of the law who came down from Jerusalem said, "He is possessed by Beelzebul! By the prince of demons, he is driving out demons."

²³ So Jesus called them over to him and began to speak to them in parables: "How can Satan drive out Satan? ²⁴ If a kingdom is divided against itself, that kingdom cannot stand. ²⁵ If a house is divided against itself, that house cannot stand. ²⁶ And if Satan opposes himself and is divided, he cannot stand; his end has come.

Jesus knew Satan was real. How about you, Reader? Do you know Satan is real?

He has desires **(Luke22:31)**, and he has a spirit of lust **(Jn 8:44)** ⁴⁴ You belong to your father, the devil, and you want to carry out your father's desires. He was a murderer from the beginning, not holding to the truth, for there is no truth in him. When he lies, he speaks his native language, for he is a liar and the father of lies.

There are so many other things that could be written about him alone that could make a book of itself; that is why finding the right Church that teaches and preaches these things is so important. Lastly, you must understand how this all pans out.

Satan was created by Christ along with all other principalities and powers in heaven in earth **(Col 1:15-18)**. ¹⁵ The Son is the image of the invisible God, the firstborn over all creation. ¹⁶ For in him all things were created: things in heaven and on earth, visible and invisible, whether thrones or powers or rulers or authorities; all things have been created through him and for him. [17] He is before all things, and in him all things hold together.

Also, what most believer don't know that Lucifer before he became Satan was the first ruler of the earth not Adam**(Isa 14:12-14 Eze 28:11-17)**, he is the enemy of good and the accuser of man **(Mt 13:28)**, he is the first sinner, the first rebel as mentioned in **Isa 14:12-14**, he is cunning **(2 Cor2:11)**, wicked **(Jn 8:44)** he is malignant like a cancer **(Luke 8:12)** [12] Those along the path are the ones who hear, and then the devil comes and takes away the word from their hearts, so that they may not believe and be saved.

He is cowardly **(James4:7)**, a thief **(John 10:10)**, he is without principle and takes advantage of men in their weakest moments **(2 Cor2: 10-11)** [10] Anyone you forgive, I also forgive. And what I have forgiven—if there was anything to forgive—I have forgiven in the sight of Christ for your sake, [11] in order that Satan might not outwit us, for we are not unaware of his schemes.

He tries to overload the mind with convictions and depression and regret, making you feel undeserving of God's grace, his love, his forgiveness towards your wrongs, remember he is a Liar and the Father of Lies! God Loves HE forgives!

Satan even goes as far as to "appears as an angel of light to deceive men" **(2 Cor 11:14)**, he is aggressive **(Eph 4:27)** in using ever method conceivable to keep men from God and in subjection to him, if he fails to do this then he tries to kill your testimony of what God has done for you, to ruin your influence with God.

If a person falls, he tries to cause him to hurt himself or even commit suicide to stay fallen, he tries to get others in a melancholy state so that God will eventually cut them off in the end.

He brings damnable heresies to lead men to rebellion against God **(2 Pet. 2:1)**. He preaches sermons and uses all the influences possible through fallen men, fallen angels, and demons, to get men to stay away from God, and that causes them to sin.

He is the author of all false religions and never discourages men in following them, for he knows this is the one way that he is sure to dam their souls.

He tries to cause men to end their lives by making them think that this is the best way out, but he hides the fact that this will only be the beginning of real torment in eternal Hell.

He dares men to do things that they would not do under ordinary circumstances. He makes young people think that they are missing everything in life if they do not go into all kinds of sins that will damn their souls. He highlights sin in such a way that makes them think and feel it's pleasurable. He stirs unholy passions in them and causes them to throw away all restraints and live a life partying, sex, drugs, music, in some cases leading to violence, occults.

He makes them think that serving God is boring, that there's no joy in it, that it's for lames. This is his greatest weapon, a lie! Serving Christ and winning souls for the kingdom will pay the greatest return investment ever.

Young people should get right with God, taste and see how good the Lord truly is, and experience the glory of salvation. Then they will be able to hear God resist the devil and not go into sin and shame.

Satan also gives seminars to businessmen, and he is their life coach, preaching that all they need to focus on is taking their entire lifetime to focus on getting rich before serving the Lord, and most respond, "I'm trying to get myself right first!"

Satan knows that the word of God outlines a life of prosperity and abundance with God's help.

He uses Church leaders, with fancy titles to make religion a paying proposition and institution that focuses on appealing to rich and influential people, to make salvation easy for all, to lower the standard of the Bible on holy living, to become formal and outward in Christian worship and living, to compromise the essentials of the faith, to preach currents events and have book reviews in the pulpit instead of preaching the gospel that will save the soul, to justify the sins and unholy lives of church members and to be as much like the world as possible in order to attract the world.

There is no realm which Satan does not seek to control, and he will never be satisfied until as he has deceived as many people as possible, and they are in eternal Hell, and God is defeated in blessing all men everywhere with all the good things of life. He uses the distortion that there are so many Religions to argue that one cannot tell which is right.

Angels/ Demons and fallen Angels.

Now we shall discover what we should know about Satan, angels, fallen angels, and demons, and how all this interacts. Bear with me. The first thing we need to know about the Satan Angels is:

They are "Sinful and rebellious," **Job 4:18. Jude 6;7 2 Peter 2:4**.

They are "to be punished," **Isaiah 24:21**

In that day the LORD will punish the powers in the heavens above and the kings on the earth below.

Isaiah 25: 7http://biblehub.com/isaiah/25-7.htm

On this mountain, he will destroy the shroud that enfolds all peoples, the sheet that covers all nations.

They "deceive Men" **2 Corinthians 11:4**

4 For if someone comes to you and preaches a Jesus other than the Jesus we preached, or if you receive a different spirit from the Spirit you received, or a different gospel from the one you accepted, you put up with it easily enough.

They Know how to preach!

They "Oppose us" according to **Romans 8:38,39**

38 For I am convinced that neither death nor life, neither angels nor demons,[k] neither the present nor the future, nor any powers, 39 neither height nor depth, nor anything else in all creation, will be able to separate us from the love of God that is in Christ Jesus our Lord.

They try to separate us from our power source! Christ and the Church!

They "fell with Lucifer." **Revelation 12:3-4** Then another sign appeared in Heaven: an enormous red dragon with seven heads and ten horns and seven crowns on its heads. 4. His tail swept a third of the stars out of the sky and flung them to the earth. The Dragon stood in front of the woman (earth) who was about to give birth (Christ and then comes the Church then comes salvation and the Power) so that it may devour her child the moment it was born.

Fallen Angels, Not Demons

There are two classes of Angels, according to scripture.

They are "organized into principalities and powers," meaning they have structure.

Ephesians 3:10

New International Version

[10] His intent was that now, through the church, the manifold wisdom of God should be made known to the rulers and authorities in the heavenly realms,

It was given to the Church by GOD.

When the church wakes up and realizes that God places the same authority and powers that Christ gives to his angels to fight in the heavenly realms, we have the same authority on the earth through the CHURCH! That is why the devil fights to destroy the image of the Church and those who lead it.

Satan's number one mission is to disconnect you from your Power source, HIS, blood and HIS Testimony! What is it? That he defeated Satan and took back what he stole from Adam.

By now, you, the reader, can see that there are things moving and happening in the current stage we exist in, and one past, present, and a future to come. You now understand the war we are in, where will you end up? Back to the invisible realm.

Now let us look at and examine the two classes of fallen angels:

Those that are bound according to **Revelation 9 verse 7-14**

[7] The locusts looked like horses prepared for battle. On their heads they wore something like crowns of gold, and their faces resembled human faces. [8] Their hair was like women's hair, and their teeth were like lions' teeth. [9] They had breastplates like breastplates of iron, and

the sound of their wings was like the thundering of many horses and chariots rushing into battle. ¹⁰ They had tails with stingers, like scorpions, and in their tails, they had power to torment people for five months. ¹¹ They had as king over them the angel of the Abyss, whose name in Hebrew is Abaddon and in Greek is Apollyon (that is, Destroyer).

Notice the scripture says, "they are prepared for battle" and "they had power to torment people." Demons are in prison, but soon they will be released on the earth when the river Euphrates is dried up!

Then Peter tells us in **2 Peter 2 verse 4**:

2 Peter 2:4

New International Version

⁴ For if God did not spare angels when they sinned, but sent them to hell, putting them in chains of darkness to be held for judgment;

If GOD did not spare the angels, he will not spare the Humans!

Jude also states:

⁶ And the angels who did not keep their positions of authority but abandoned their proper dwelling—these he has kept in darkness, bound with everlasting chains for judgment on the great Day. ⁷ In a similar way, Sodom and Gomorrah and the surrounding towns gave themselves up to sexual immorality and perversion. They serve as an example of those who suffer the punishment of eternal fire.

Here are the stakes: we either believe what is written and take the steps to escape this coming Judgement, and believe me, it will come! Or we can give man credit for being so smart and deceiving with their human knowledge and religious lies and deception that will soon cause the death of millions. You, reader, can help get involved in the battle.

The bounds angels are being held to accomplish GOD'S final plan.

They will be "cast out of Heaven and will fight against Christ at Armageddon." **Revelations (12: 7-9)**

[7] Then war broke out in heaven. Michael and his angels fought against the dragon, and the dragon and his angels fought back. [8] But he was not strong enough, and they lost their place in heaven. [9] The great dragon was hurled down—that ancient serpent called the devil, or Satan, who leads the whole world astray. He was hurled to the earth, and his angels with him.

Notice that a war breaks out, and Michael and His Angels fought against Satan the Dragon and his angels, and they fought back. But the Satan was not strong enough, and they lost their place in heaven. I want you to understand that most Christians err in the fact that Jesus, the son of God, is not the one fighting Satan, but Michael the Archangel is, but why?

Because Christ is seated at the right hand with the Father, far above all realms and dominions, and he has already defeated Satan on the Cross, now he gives Power to the Church and Prince Michael and his angels through HIS Blood and their Testimony!

Introduction of the Son

HE SPEAKS: Marvin, imagine if a person had a son. And did not give him a name? But just called him son? What would be his name? How would the father call him and talk to him? Would he need a name if the father were the only one speaking to him?

Me: No, I said I imagine not.

Voice: Is the son a real person? even though he has no name? And if people were to ask? Who is this and I reply" this is my son! Is the son real?

And a voice from heaven said, "This is my Son, whom I love; with him I am well pleased." (Scriptures added by me). **Matthew 3:17.**

Me: yes Lord!

Voice: "No man come to the father, except through my son whom I have chosen to redeem them"

John 14:6

"Jesus answered, "I am the way, the truth, and the life. No one comes to the father except through me." (Scriptures added by me).

Voice: Tell them that this is what the Lord Almighty has declared, write, and put in a book!

ME: Yes, Lord, and may people everywhere who read "Be strengthened, learn, and receive your salvation, grace, and your Mercy and YOUR SON.

I feel the simplicity of the questions, it sounds like one from someone on a more personal level, like a Father speaking regarding HIS SON.

Humans want to dictate who God chooses to endow with Power, and who he gives authority to. Satan himself leads this dictation.

Colossians 1:16 For by Him all things were created that are in heaven and that are on earth, visible and invisible, whether thrones, dominions, principalities, or powers. All things were created through Him (Jesus, Gods Son) and for Him.

The Him is his Son Jesus.

What if, in our own limited imagination, God chose to name "Son" as a name and not just a title that we identify with? But to grasp and accept even that idea, we must first recognize the term "son" can only come from what we recognize in association with a family. Maybe not how we define family, a Husband/Father, Wife/Mother, and children. According to Merriam-Webster's definition, **a family is a group of individuals living under one roof and usually under one head.**

So already we see that if God said, "Let us make man in our image and in our likeness?" Wouldn't that also speak to his family? He said "our." I believe the problem we have is that we cannot phantom the idea of family without thinking of reproduction in forms of sex. And yet Christ would still come through the creation process that God designed, and he would not violate it.

Matthew 1:23

Behold, a virgin shall be with child, and shall bring forth a son, and they shall call his name Emmanuel, which being interpreted is, God with us.

Notice the scripture says, "and they." They who? The answer: Humans shall call him Emmanuel.

Isn't it funny that no one has a problem with the name "Emmanue.l"

Even Mary was confused about how this would happen, since she had never known a man.

Luke Chapter 1 verse 34-37

And Mary said to the angel, "How shall this be, since I have no husband?" And the angel said to her, "The Holy Spirit will come upon you, and the power of the Highest will overshadow you; therefore, the child to be born will be called holy, the Son of God. And behold, your kinswoman Elizabeth in her old age has also conceived a son; and this is the sixth month with her who was called barren. For with God nothing will be impossible."

It is not realistic to believe that a human could produce a God child unless a power greater than what we can explain, with details we cannot describe, takes over. The angel said something many humans struggle with "For with God nothing will be impossible."

Notice that John the Baptist was also supernatural; Elizabeth, in her Old age, had also conceived a Son, but no one argues the validity of John's birth or his name, which was also given by the messenger from heaven. Although Zechariah was John's natural father, he was well beyond reproductive age, and again we see that John's child was the answer to his prayer.

Luke 1:13

English Standard Version

But the angel said to him, "Do not be afraid, Zechariah, for your prayer has been heard, and your wife Elizabeth will bear you a son, and you shall call his name John."

The angel said, "And you shall call his name John."

And what about Sarah Abraham's wife:

English Standard Version

God said, "No, but Sarah your wife shall bear you a son, and you shall call his name Isaac. I will establish my covenant with him as an everlasting covenant for his offspring after him."

Notice again, but this time God said, "You shall call his name Isaac."

But no one questions Isaac, birth his name nothing?

Sarah Laughs at the Promise Genesis 18:9-11

⁹"Where is your wife, Sarah?" they asked. "There, in the tent," he replied. ¹⁰Then the LORD said, "I will surely return to you at this time next year, and your wife Sarah will have a son!" Now Sarah was behind him, listening at the entrance to the tent. ¹¹And Abraham and Sarah were already old and well along in years; Sarah had passed the age of childbearing....

Berean Standard Bible

And yet no one dispute the birth of Isaac or his name?

Sarah Laughs at the Promise

...¹³And the LORD asked Abraham, "Why did Sarah laugh and say, 'Can I really bear a child when I am old?' ¹⁴Is anything too difficult for the LORD? At the appointed time I will return to you— in about a year — and Sarah will have a son." ¹⁵But Sarah was afraid, so she denied it and said, "I did not laugh." "No," replied the LORD, "but you did laugh."

Again, we hear "Is there anything too difficult for the LORD?'

Sarah did the same thing that most people do. God says he is going to do something. Then our natural mind tries to understand something we cannot, we laugh, we doubt, we hesitate, we pause, we fear, we question, we do not believe, we discredit.

Jesus and the Samaritan Woman

John 4:21-,23

...²¹"Believe Me, woman," Jesus replied, "a time is coming when you will worship the Father neither on this mountain nor in Jerusalem. ²²You worship what you do not know; we worship what we do know, for salvation is from the Jews.

²³But a time is coming and has now come when the true worshipers will worship the Father in spirit and in truth, for the Father is seeking such as these to worship him."

I am starting to believe that meditating is so much different than prayer; it is more about silencing the world from every distraction and idea of the mind and entering a place of inner heaven.

Here is a revelation for you, reader, God has the ability and the authority to change names:

Revelation 2:17 Whoever has ears, let them hear what the Spirit say to the churches. To the one who is victorious, I will give some of the hidden manna. I will also give that person a white stone with a new name written on it, known only to the one who receives it.

God changes names!

Revelation 3:12 The one who is victorious I will make a new pillar in the temple of my God. Never again will they leave it. I will (Jesus' speaking) I will write on them the name of my God and the name of the city of my God, the new Jerusalem, which is coming down out of heaven from my God, and I will also write on them MY NEW NAME. Jesus gets a new name! **Many Religious people do not even know that his name has changed, I believe, because we will no longer need salvation because we have been redeemed.**

Jesus had the same authority to change names; I say unto you are Peter (which means rock), **Matthew 16:18**

Jacob's name was also changed in **Genesis 32:28**: "Your name is Jacob, but you will no longer be called Jacob; your name will be Israel."

How about Abram? **Genesis 17:5 NLT** What is more, I am changing your name. It will no longer be Abram. Instead, you will be called Abraham, for you will be the father of many nations.

Jesus said- I was sent to do my father's will, I only speak the words of my father, no one has seen the father but the only begotten son, in my father house are many mansions, when he prayed, he said "Our Father," and" Father into thy hands," not my will but thy will be done. It can never be clearer that, while on this earth, Jesus was in communication with someone. That somebody was his father.

I believe God took something so simple to show us images of himself: we were made in his image and his likeness; we can create things in our own image and likeness. We call them children. But when God said this is my son? No way, God? You are too impressive to be Holy, to great, to wonderful, too Magnificent to have an equal? We think we flatter God with words, but we offend him by not accepting his words.

Because our human brain is so conditioned to naming everything either after someone or ourselves, what if a father had a son for years that had no name? Seems odd and a little strange, but it is the father's right. People have been getting the wrong Idea about God the same way. They have taken attributes of God and given the attribute a name, and worship the attribute, not God. People have been divided and have even murdered each other because of it.

The Father speaks; Respect My name!

Reade, God is so beyond our comprehension; HE is so Holy that we cannot even say HIS name the wrong way. We wonder why HE must use different names, so that we can use names to help our understanding in describing an action or something that God is doing on the earth. God protects HIS name to protect us, as we see later when Moses is given the Laws

GOD gives a name to introduce His Law! The name "I AM!"

And God said moreover to Moses, thus shall you say to the children of Israel, Jehovah, the God of your fathers, the God of Abraham, the God of Isaac, and the God of Jacob, has sent me to you: This is my name for ever; and this is MY memorial to all Generations **(Exodus 3;13-15)** thereafter God used the name Jehovah to begin the work of the Law through Moses. Moses knew that people would ask him what HIS name was because he was going back down to a Land that was serving other gods. The gods of Egypt. This is why in the commandments the ONE TRUE GOD said something that most people think offends HIM? That there are other gods.

Thou shalt have no other Gods before me. Neither shall thou bow down nor worship them!

Unfortunately, that command was broken, which meant a new name would have to be given to redeem us. So let us take the journey together.

"You shall not take the name of the Lord (your God) in vain." **(Exodus 20:7 -Third Commandment)**.

"In vain" means "iniquity," "falsehood," "vanity," "emptiness." Reverence is the chief purpose of the third commandment **(Psalm 111:9; Eccl. 5:1, 2)**. Those who serve none but the true GOD, and serve HIM in spirit and in truth, will avoid any careless, irreverent, or unnecessary use of the holy name. The careless use of God's name denotes a lack of reverence for HIM. If our thinking is on a spiritually elevated plane, our words will also be elevated and dictated by what is honest and sincere **(Philippians 4:8)**.

Imagine how many times you have heard someone swearing using God in reference.

<u>New King James Version</u>

Exodus 3:15

And God said to Moses, "I AM WHO I AM."

And He said, "Thus you shall say to the children of Israel, 'I AM has sent me to you.'"

Exodus 20:3 Context

[1]And God spake all these words, saying, [2]I am the LORD thy God, which have brought thee out of the land of Egypt, out of the house of bondage, [3] thou shall serve no other Gods [4]Thou shalt not make unto thee any graven image, or any likeness of anything that is in heaven above, or that is in the earth beneath, or that is in the water under the earth: [5]Thou shalt not bow down thyself to them, nor serve them: for I the LORD thy God am a jealous God, visiting the iniquity of the fathers upon the children unto the third and fourth generation of them that hate me; [6]And shewing mercy unto thousands of them that love me, and keep my commandments.

Here is what the One true God said about Him and other Gods!

Deuteronomy 6:5 – *"And thou shalt love the LORD thy God with all thine heart, and with all thy soul, and with all thy might."*

Psalms 81:9 – *"There shall no strange god be in thee; neither shalt thou worship any strange god."*

Notice he said no God is allowed to be in thee!

Exodus 20:23 – *"Ye shall not make anything to be with me gods of silver, neither shall ye make unto you gods of gold you shall not make for yourselves."*

Isaiah 44:8 – *"Fear ye not, neither be afraid: have not I told thee from that time and have declared it? Ye are even my witnesses. Is there a God beside me? Yea, there is no GOD; I know not any."*

Isaiah 45:21-22 – *"Tell ye, and bring them near; yea, let them take counsel together: who hath declared this from ancient time? who hath told it from that time? have not I the LORD? and there is no God else beside me; a just God and a Saviour; there is none beside me. Look unto me, and be ye saved, all the ends of the earth: for I am God, and there is none else.   "*

Isaiah 46:9 – *"Remember the former things of old: for I am God, and there is none else; I am God, and there is none like me,"*

Matthew 4:10 – *"Then saith Jesus unto him, get thee hence, Satan: for it is written, thou shalt worship the Lord thy God, and him only shalt thou serve."*

1 Corinthians 8:4 – *"As concerning therefore the eating of those things that are offered in sacrifice unto idols, we know that an idol is nothing in the world, and that there is none other God but one."*

1 Corinthians 8:6 – *"But to us there is but one God, the Father, of whom are all things, and we in him; and one Lord Jesus Christ, by whom are all things, and we by him."*

Philippians 3:19 – *"Whose end is destruction, whose God is their belly, and whose glory is in their shame, who mind earthly things."*

God clearly declares that HE alone is God, and there is no other besides him; nothing made, imagined, or created.

Man, in all his attempts, cannot refute the God of I AM.

Acts 17: 24- 32 Paul speaking to the religious people of the day:

[24] The God who made the world and everything in it, being Lord of heaven and earth, does not live in temples made by man,[a] [25] nor is he served by human hands, as though he needed anything, since he himself gives to all mankind life and breath and everything. [26] And he made from one man every nation of mankind to live on all the face of the earth, having determined allotted periods and the boundaries of their dwelling place, [27] that they should seek God, and perhaps feel their way toward him and find him. Yet he is not far from each one of us, [28] for "'In him we live and move and have our being'; as even some of your own poets have said, "'For we are indeed his offspring. [29] Being then God's offspring, we ought not to think that the divine being is like gold or silver or stone, an image formed by the art and imagination of man. [30] The times of ignorance God overlooked, but now he commands all people everywhere to repent, [31] because he has fixed a day on which he will judge the world in righteousness by a man whom he has appointed; and of this he has given assurance to all by raising him from the dead."

[32] Now when they heard of the resurrection of the dead, some mocked. But others said, "We will hear you again about this." [33] So Paul went out from their midst. [34] But some men joined him and believed, among whom also were Dionysius the Areopagite and a woman named Damaris and others with them.

Most Christians are offended when people say that they serve other gods; hearing that does not bother me because I know the God of Abraham, the God of Isaac, the God of Jacob. So, God was basically sending Moses to Egypt to pick a fight with the Gods of Egypt; every God was represented from the land, to the animals, crops, the Nile River, the air, skin, body and health, weather, sea, and even life and death, and the LORD GOD ALMIGHTY proved that he was master over them all.

By now, man was becoming more and more sinful; the first [39] books of the Bible are nothing more than man's failed attempt to obey the

God who said I AM THAT I AM. From Genesis all the way to the book of Malachi, from all the prophets, and all the Kings, great men and women alike were not able to redeem man, by obeying his law to perfection, until the book of Matthew starts with the" birth of Christ was on this wise." God had a Son, who would be like Adam, but live on the earth and be without sin.

Redemption must be made for mankind, yet man continues to dictate the terms of God's requirements.

Confusion creates most of the arguments; man, in his attempts to serve God, does quite the opposite. Man will kill for their beliefs and even persecute others with different beliefs than theirs, but GOD is the one who makes the rules for us to follow, and HE alone determines what he shall be called, how he shall be served and worship, not Man or their aggressive attempts, and all their education or concocted dreams and imaginations.

And the God I am referring to does not need Man to fight for Him or to kill others who reject Him; He alone will deal with them; it is not Man's job. Names does not make a Religion or a God. I believe that Satan, along with the help of people use names, race, gender, and color them to refute others' ideas to control them. Let us look at Names and how they have confused people.

Because a person did a certain task did not make it a Religion; for example, John the Baptist is what he was known for, not his Religion. The Apostles were made that way by Christ; that did not create a religion; they were at Pentecost. That did not make them Pentecostal. Most Religions received their names and identities from men, not from God. God did not create religions; man did. God created a plan of redemption through salvation.

Old Testament Names of God

In this chapter, I will deal with the names of God, and you tell me whether they warrant making a Religion of.

The first name is ***Elohim***. This is the Hebrew word for God in Genesis 1:1 and appears in 3,000 other places in the Old Testament. It is a unipersonal noun meaning "Gods" and is so translated 239 times; it is the plural of ElOAH, meaning "deity" and "God". It is used in the plural with the definite article of the Supreme God. It is translated "judges" in **(Exodus 21;6, 22:8-9)** and "angels" **(PS 8:5)**.

Sometimes ***Elohim*** is used in connection with plural verbs and pronouns, as seen in the Hebrew text **(Genesis 20:13)**, "the Gods, they caused me to wander" and in **Genesis 35:7**, "there the Gods they appeared unto him," Many times plurals pronouns are used of God in referring to the different members of the Godhead," as "us" **(Gen.1:26; 3:22; 11:7; Isa 6:8; Jn,17:21)**, "our" **(Gen1:26; Jn14. v23)**, "We" Jn.14:23; 17:11,22 and "their" Ps2:3.

First-, second-, and third-person pronouns are used hundreds of times in Scripture to refer to one, two, or three persons in the deity. Some of these are used of men, concerning different members of the deity, and of each other. In John 17 alone, Jesus uses 162 pronouns in speaking to and of his Father. In Psalms 119, there are 610 pronouns used of man to and of God. Other chapters in the Bible use many like pronouns, and they are all used correctly and should be understood in the same sense in connection with God as when they are used of other subjects.

When different members of the deity speak to and of each other, just like men do, should we accuse them of misrepresenting themselves and of not being able to use the human language properly? We have more right to believe that only one person is referred to when men use first, second, and third personal singular and plural pronouns of and to each other, as to believe there is only one person referred to when the members of the Godhead use them of and to each other.

When singular pronouns are used of deity, it is one of the three persons of the Trinity speaking of Himself or as representing of the Godhead, or it is one of the three divine persons speaking to another one concerning a third person of the Trinity, as it is clear in John 14:16-17.

16 And I will ask the Father, and he will give you another advocate to help you and be with you forever—17 the Spirit of truth. The world cannot accept HIM, because it neither sees HIM nor knows HIM. But you know HIM, for HE lives with you and will be in you.

In the Old Testament, it was the Father who was the prominent speaker **(Hebrews 1:1-3; Acts 3:21)**; in the gospels, the Son was the prominent speaker **(John 17:8)**; and now it is the Holy Spirit who is the prominent speaker. **(John 14:26)**.

Singular pronouns are used of the whole Godhead as a unit **(Exodus 20:3)** just like the whole church as the body of Christ as a unit spoken of as a "man" and "he" as in **(Ephesians 4:11-13)**

Pay close attention to this scripture 11So Christ himself gave the apostles, the prophets, the evangelists, the pastors, and teachers, to equip HIS people for works or service, not for HIS people to serve them.

The one *Elohim*, then, is not one person or one in number, but one in unity. *Elohim* is not a divided deity but, but three persons in "one God" or one deity. The word itself does not say there are three, but merely that deity is plural. God is thus referred to in the plural twice as often as the word "Jesus" is found in both Testaments.

Elohim- three persons one God

YEHOVAH means "the self -existent," "Eternal and Immutable One," or "Unity." – JEHOVAH {Not a Religion or Denomination}

EL. -The Hebrew word for God- means "the strong one" or "*Elohim the Omnipotent,*" thus, *Elohim* is "God the creator" {Not a Religion or Denomination}

ELOAH- This is the Hebrew word for "God" that is found 56 times in scripture. It is "Elohim who is to be worshipped." It is the name of God when worshipped as an idol, contrasted with worship of the true God. It is "the living God "in contrast to dead gods. It means "deity" and "God." {Not a Religion or Denomination}

ELYON, The Hebrew word that means "Most High" and is also translated 40 times in scripture that means "the Supreme" the Highest," "Highest" "Lofty."

It is *EL*, the possessor of Heaven and Earth, and *Elohim*, the creator of Heaven and Earth. Note that Jesus is never called the Most High, but the Son of the Most High God **(Mark 5:7)**, He (Demon) shouted at the top of his voice, "What do you want with me, *Jesus, Son of the "Most High God"*? The demon recognized HIM as the *Son of THE MOST-HIGH GOD* he knew Jesus had authority and power as The SON and as GOD and wanted no confrontation at all!"

The Angels during the birth of Christ sang "Glory to God in the Highest," who was not Jesus **(Luke 2:14)**. According to scripture in **(1 Cor 11:3)**, the Father is still the "head of Christ"; so, he is rightfully the *Highest God* {Again not a Religion or a Denomination}

ADON. This is the Hebrew word for "Lord," and is translated 195 times in the Old Testament. It means "Sovereign," "Ruler," "Master." *Adonai* is the emphatic form of *Adon* and is translated "Lord," 430 times in the Old Testament. There are two *Adonais* mentioned in Ps:110;1 The Lord says to my lord: "Sit at my right hand until {I} make {your} enemies a footstool for {your} feet."

Notice he did not say,"My feet."

A few other times the names of God in the Old Testament are "*JAH*" (Ps. 68:4, 18); "I AM THAT I AM" and "I AM" (Exod.3:13-15);

"God Almighty" **(Exod. 6:3)** "Lord God" **(Gen. 2:4 and hundreds of times)**; "Jealous"**(Exod.34:14)**: "The Lord of Host"**(Isa47:4 and 281 other times)**; "Holy"**(Isa 57:15)**; and many other names, thus proving the doctrine that "Jesus" is the only God and the only name of that God is unscriptural.

If God said these were His names, and some beings say they are not, who do we believe? Some believe that these names are titles signifying office, rank, or relationship, but this is more of a human theory and contradicts the scriptures, which say they are real names.

The Attributes of God

He has an Angel:

[7] The angel of the LORD found Hagar near a spring in the desert; it was the spring that is beside the road to Shur.[8] And he said, "Hagar, slave of Sarai, where have you come from, and where are you going?"

"I'm running away from my mistress Sarai," she answered.

[9] Then the ***angel of the LORD told her***, "Go back to your mistress and submit to her." [10] The angel added, "I will increase your descendants so much that they will be too numerous to count."

[11] The ***angel of the LORD also said*** to her:

"You are now pregnant and you will give birth to a son.

You shall name him Ishmael,[a] for the LORD has heard of your misery.

[12] He will be a wild donkey of a man; his hand will be against everyone and everyone's hand against him, and he will live in hostility toward[b] all his brothers."

[13] She gave this name to the LORD who spoke to her: "You are the God who sees me," for she said, "I have now seen[c] the One who sees me." [14] That is why the well was called Beer Lahai Roi[d]; it is still there, between Kadesh and Bered.

Now I will list some of the attributes of God that many have either made a Religion or a Characteristic or personality of God that fits their own understanding. Let us review what the Bible says:

Psalms 93:1-5, The Lord reigns, he is robed in majesty; the Lord is robed in majesty and armed with strength; indeed, the world is established, firm and secure.

2 Your throne was established long ago; you are from all eternity.

3 The seas have lifted, Lord, the seas have lifted their voice; the seas have lifted their pounding waves.

4 Mightier than the thunder of the great waters; mightier than the breakers of the sea-the Lord on high is mighty,

5 Your statutes, Lord; stand firm; holiness adorns your house for endless days.

Isaiah 44: 6-8 This is what the Lord says – Israel King and Redeemer, the Lord Almighty: *I am the first and the Last; apart from me there is no God.*

7 *Who then is like me*? Let him proclaim it. Let him declare and lay out before me what has happened since I established my ancient people, and what is yet to come- yes, let them foretell what will come.

8 Do not tremble, do not be afraid. Did I not proclaim this and foretell this long ago? You are my witnesses. *Is there any God besides me? No there is no other Rock; I know not one.*

Many times, *God declares himself as the creator of the worlds* in **Genesis1:1-2** In the beginning God created the heavens and the earth. 2 Now the earth was formless and empty, darkness was over the face of the deep, and the Spirit of God was hovering over the waters.

Also, **Genesis:1 verse 25**: God made the wild animals according to their kinds, the livestock according to their kind, and all the creatures that move along the ground according to their kinds, and God saw that it was good.

He Has a Council:

And the most awesome scripture I ever read in the bible **Psalms 89; verse 5-8**

5 The heavens praise your wonders, Lord your faithfulness too, *IN THE ASSEMBLY OF THE HOLY ONES (the other Gods)* 6 For who in the skies above can compare with the Lord? *Who is like the Lord among the heavenly beings? 7 In the council of the Holy ones, God is greatly feared; he is more awesome than all who surround him. 8 Who is like you, Lord God Almighty? You, Lord is mighty, and your faithfulness surrounds you.*

God sits in an Assembly of other Gods. He also has a council, so it is said that God judges no one. He has a council that knows him, fears him, and knows that he is righteous, and they, I believe, render decisions in some matters in Heaven?

Hebrews:1-verse 3 The Son (notice he does not mention a name?) Is the radiance of God's glory and the exact representation of his being, sustaining all things by his powerful word. After he had provided purification of sins, *he (Jesus) sat down at the right hand of majesty in heaven.* If it is not clear now, God is not to be underestimated, feared, or revered. He has ALL Power and can do what he wants; man just has not come to accept this.

Although many have rejected the name, I have given them to be saved; many will not be saved because they argue over a name, not His Attributes, which reveal that he is mine and we are one. Many are in disbelief because of his name and yet many do believe and many of them will be just as shocked when he receives a new name according to the book of **Revelations 2:17** *"He that hath an ear, let them hear what the Spirit saith unto the churches; To him that over cometh will I give to eat of the hidden manna, and will give him a white stone, and in the stone a NEW NAME written, which no man it's saving her that received it."*

He has a council of other Gods:

In the book of Kings **(1 Kings 22:19)**, The I saw the Lord sitting on his throne; so, it was presented to his mind, as if he had seen with his bodily eyes the divine Being in a glorious form, as a king sitting on his throne, to do justice and judgment; as Ahab and Jehoshaphat were now sitting on their thrones, only as a far greater King, even the King of kings, and in a more splendid manner: and all the host of heaven standing by him on his right hand and on his left the ministering angels ready to do his will.

Isaiah 6:8-9

New King James Version

8 Also I heard the voice of the Lord, saying:

"Whom shall I send,

And who will go for Us?"

Then I said, "Here am I! Send me."

9 "And He said, 'Go, and tell this people 'Keep on hearing, but do not understand; Keep on seeing, but do not perceive.'"

Jeremiah 23:21-22

New King James Version

21 "I have not sent these prophets, yet they ran. I have not spoken to them, yet they prophesied."

22 "But if they had stood in My counsel, and had caused My people to hear My words, then they would have turned them from their evil way and from the evil of their doings."

Job 15:8

New King James Version

[8] *"Have you heard the counsel of God?* Do you limit wisdom to yourself?"

A Psalm of Asaph.

[82] "God stands in the congregation of the mighty; *He judges among the gods."*

He has a Spirit:

<u>King James Bible</u>

"For God hath not given us the spirit of fear; but of power, and of love, and of a sound mind."

Isaiah 11:2

"The Spirit of the LORD will rest on Him--the Spirit of wisdom and understanding, the Spirit of counsel and strength, the Spirit of knowledge and fear of the LORD."

Romans 8:15

"For ye have not received the spirit of bondage again to fear; but ye have received the Spirit of adoption, whereby we cry, Abba, Father."

Zechariah 4:6

"Then he answered and spake unto me, saying, this is the word of the LORD unto Zerubbabel, saying, not by might, nor by power, but by my spirit, saith the LORD of host."

And finally, **Luke 12-8-10** "And I say to you, everyone who confesses Me before men, the Son of Man will confess before the Father, the son of man will confess him also before the angels of God," 9 but he who denies Me before men, will be denied before the angels of God. 10 And everyone who speaks a word against the Son of Man, it will be forgiven him; but he who blasphemes against the Holy Spirit, it will not be forgiven him."

He Has a Son:

Now I will close out my short writing with the following final thoughts. So far, we have reviewed the mistakes often associated with *"The LORD GOD ALMIGHTY."* Many have used and debated just about every issue under the sun to refute the existence of God. But people change their names all the time, give themselves nicknames, stage names, alias all the time. People will also delegate power and authority all the time, especially in families. When a couple shares time together, they begin to grow as one; they think the same, can finish each other's sentences, and know each other's favorite foods, colors, fears, as well as joys and pleasures. When this happens, they begin to feel a sense of oneness and can often be heard saying, "We are one."

Yet when Jesus says, Me and My Father are One, or you hear there are three that bear witness in Heaven, the Father, the Son, and the Holy Spirit. There must be a major debate to refute his words.

The term "the Holy Ghost" is not applied to men, or to the Father or to the Son, but only and always to the third person of the Godhead, who proceeds from the Father and the Son. It only makes me more curious about the things associated with God; <u>He has his own Angel</u>, **Exodus 23:20,21**, Brenton Septuagint Translation:

20 *"And behold, I send My angel before thy face, that he may keep thee in the way, that he may bring thee into the land which I have prepared for thee."*

21 *"Take heed to thyself and hearken to him and disobey him not; for he will not give way to thee, for my name is on him."*

He has a son.

Luke 9:36 *Then a voice from the cloud said, "<u>This is my son, my chosen One</u>, listen to him,"*

Final Meditation Creation

God, the creator of all things, as we have seen, the God of the Spiritual, Natural, Animal, and the Plant World, the God of the Oceans and the Solar systems and the heavens and the earth and all that exist on them, has one creation I would like to end with; and that the inner man he created in us all. Many, unfortunately, will never get to meet the one inside of us, who I believe can only be heard in meditation. Let us examine.

1 Peter 3: verse 4 reads

[4] rather *let it be* the hidden person of the heart, with the incorruptible *beauty* of a gentle and quiet spirit, which is very precious in the sight of God.

God has created a person who lives in our hearts.

2 Corinthians 4 verse 16 New King James Version

[16] Therefore we do not lose heart. Even though our outward man is perishing, yet the inward *man* is being renewed day by day.

Even though we are constantly aging and dying daily, and getting older, there is an inner man who is getting stronger and stronger, preparing himself for eternity. The question is: how will your inner man spend it? The choice is up to you!

Proverbs 20: 27 New King James Version

The spirit of a man is the lamp of the LORD,
Searching all the inner depths of his heart.

It is the inner man who tells God all things concerning us and I believe God judges the words that come out of our mouth versus the words that he hears from the inner man, the inner man in honest, pure and always tell GOD the truth, the inner man knows what we really need he intercedes and pray on our behalf, with prayers that we don't understands but he does.

Romans 8 verse 26

26 *Likewise the Spirit also helps in our weaknesses. For we do not know what we should pray for as we ought, but the Spirit Himself makes intercession for us with groanings which cannot be uttered.*

Prayer is so important because it feeds and strengthens our inner man, enabling us to make requests on our behalf to God our Father.

According to **Ephesians 3: 14-16**

[14] For this reason I bow my knees to the Father [f]of our Lord Jesus Christ, [15] from whom the whole family in heaven and earth is named, [16] that He would grant you, according to the riches of His glory, to be strengthened with might through His Spirit in the inner man/

Our strength comes from our inner man, its that man inside of you if you find him that keep you from giving up, he will keep you from failing, and he will give you peace and a direct connection to the Son of God who talks to God and the Bible says that God hears all of his prayers(the son) and the son has given us the authorization to use his name when praying to the Father.

Jesus said in the Gospel according to **John 16:24**

John 16:24-26

New King James Version

[24] *Until now you have asked nothing in My name. Ask, and you will receive, that your joy may be full.*

Jesus Christ Has Overcome the World

[25] *"These things I have spoken to you in figurative language; but the time is coming when I will no longer speak to you in figurative language, but I will tell you plainly about the Father. [26] In that day you will ask in My name, and I do not say to you that I shall pray the Father for you;"*

The Father only hears us when we ask in HIS Son's name, but we must take the initiative and pray for ourselves. Jesus will not pray; he said, "You do it."

2 Corinthians 3 verse 18 says

[18] *But we all, with unveiled face, beholding as in a mirror the glory of the Lord, are being transformed into the same image from glory to glory, just as by the Spirit of the Lord.*

The inner man is constantly being transformed into the image and likeness of God, but only as He sees Christ in the mirror in our lives.

In the book of Colossians, chapter 3, verse 10, we read:

[10] *and have put on the new man who is renewed in knowledge according to the image of Him who created him,*

The inner man discovers who and what he was created to do, as we learn the knowledge of God through his word. Our job then is to seek him out and help him discover who he is, and in return, we learn who we are.

[1] God, who [a]at various times and in various ways spoke in time past to the fathers by the prophets, [2] has in these last days spoken to us by His Son, whom He has appointed heir of all things, through whom also He made the [b]worlds; [3] who being the brightness of His glory and the express image of His person, and upholding all things by the word of His power, when He had [c]by Himself [d]purged [e]our sins, sat down at the right hand of the Majesty on high, [4] having become so much better than the angels, as He has by inheritance obtained a more excellent name than they.

Hebrews 1 verse 5-14

The Son Exalted Above Angels

⁵ *For to which of the angels did He ever say:*

"You are My Son,
Today I have begotten You"?

And again:

"I will be to Him a Father,
And He shall be to Me a Son"?

⁶ *But when He again brings the firstborn into the world, He says:*

"Let all the angels of God worship Him."

⁷ *And of the angels He says:*

"Who makes His angels spirits
And His ministers a flame of fire."

⁸ *But to the Son He says:*

"Your throne, O God, is forever and ever;
A [f]scepter of righteousness is the scepter of Your kingdom.

⁹ You have loved righteousness and hated lawlessness;

Therefore God, Your God, has anointed You
With the oil of gladness more than Your companions."

¹⁰ *And:*

"You, LORD, in the beginning laid the foundation of the earth,
And the heavens are the work of Your hands.

¹¹ *They will perish, but You remain;*

And they will all grow old like a garment;

12 Like a cloak You will fold them up,

And they will be changed.
But You are the same,
And Your years will not fail."

13 But to which of the angels has He ever said:

"Sit at My right hand,
Till I make Your enemies Your footstool"?

14 Are they not all ministering spirits sent forth to minister for those who will inherit salvation.

Notice it's a conversation that the Father is having with his Son!

Salvation is waiting on you. Have you received it ? Do you know your inner man? Do you know the Father? Do you know the Son? If not, meditate on these things.

I am thankful to GOD that I know my inner man, and I hear Him, listen to Him, and know Christ the Son of God. It was His listening to the Holy Spirit that spoke directly to me to write this to you, and even if you enjoyed it, then your inner man did also. Now keep feeding him.

Thanks

Apostle Marvin D Thompkins